THE HISTORY OF WESTERN PHILOSOPHY in 100 HAIKU

First published in 2015
The Dedalus Press
13 Moyclare Road
Baldoyle
Dublin 13
Ireland

www.**dedaluspress**.com

ISBN 978 1 910251 01 0

Dedalus Press titles are represented in the UK by Central Books, 99 Wallis Road, London E9 5LN and in North America by Syracuse University Press, Inc., 621 Skytop Road, Suite 110, Syracuse, New York 13244.

Cover design: Pat Boran. Typesetting: Laura King
Printed in Ireland by Gemini International Ltd.

The Dedalus Press receives financial assistance from
The Arts Council / An Chomhairle Ealaíon

HARIS VLAVIANOS

THE HISTORY OF WESTERN PHILOSOPHY in 100 HAIKU

Translated by
Peter Mackridge

DEDALUS PRESS
DUBLIN, IRELAND

CONTENTS

AUTHOR'S INTRODUCTION

A HUNDRED PHILOSOPHERS, each one's thought condensed into seventeen syllables. It's not an easy undertaking – and it's certainly a provocative and sometimes an amusing one – for someone who sets out to marry the analytical discourse of western philosophy with the dense, minimalist form of Oriental poetry. This marriage isn't always as "sacred" as pure-blooded philosophers might like it to be; it's slightly sarcastic, as you might expect from a poet who reads philosophy in his own self-interested and always indirect way. The number 100, round as it is, is of course conventional. It could have been bigger. Nonetheless, I decided to confine myself to this convenient number, to the thinkers I've become acquainted with and whose work I've read (not always with the proper "philosophical" devotion).

Some important philosophers are absent, either because I'm not sufficiently familiar with their thought (Levinas, Bachelard, Ricoeur) or because they don't seem to have influenced the development of philosophy to the same degree as the ones I've included. And naturally, in the twentieth century, from Husserl onwards, there is (because of my education) a slight bias: sixteen Anglo-Americans as against thirteen who write in German, twelve French and one Italian. Antiquity (from the Pre-Socratics to Boethius) is represented by twenty-three names, the Middle Ages (from Avicenna to William of Ockham) by eight, the Renaissance by three, the seventeenth century by six, the eighteenth by ten, the nineteenth by eight and the twentieth by forty-two.

Under the name of each philosopher I specify the work that the haiku refers to or, in the case of the Pre-Socratics, to the relevant fragment of their work that has been preserved. I added very few notes because I didn't want the haiku to lose their potency.[1] Where my wit fails

[1] [The translator has taken the liberty of supplementing the author's notes with a few of his own, marked "PM".]

to do justice to the weighty thoughts of a philosopher, I hope I will be forgiven for my irreverence. But poetry has other ways of approaching and appropriating truth – often by way of humour.

TRANSLATOR'S INTRODUCTION

LIKE FERNANDO PESSOA, Haris Vlavianos is something of a library cataloguer's nightmare. A librarian faced with a copy of a recent edition of Bernardo Soares' *Livro do desassossego* (*Book of Disquiet*) will find no mention of Pessoa's name in the book. The only clue to the author's real identity is a tiny sketch of Pessoa with moustache, fedora, glasses and bow-tie on the front cover.

Whereas Pessoa wrote under a variety of names, Vlavianos always uses his own name on the title pages of his books. The problem for librarians is that he writes his name in two different alphabets and publishes books in unrelated disciplines. For this reason the Greek poet Χάρης Βλαβιανός (transliterated as Charēs Vlavianos according to the quaint librarians' system) and Haris Vlavianos, the author of two academic books in English on the history of resistance and civil war in Greece during the 1940s, used to be listed in the Oxford University library catalogue as two different people until I pointed out the mistake to a librarian friend.

Vlavianos's parents were Greek, but his childhood was divided between São Paolo, Rome and Athens, and he received his university education at Bristol and Oxford. As a consequence, he is conversant with the Greek, Portuguese, Italian and English languages – which partly accounts for his multiple selves and his multiple careers.

Apart from being one of Greece's leading poets, Vlavianos has two day jobs: he is poetry editor in a leading Greek publishing house and Professor of History, History of Ideas and Political Theory at the American College of Greece. In connection with his teaching post, he is currently planning a book examining the question of justice in the works of philosophers such as Plato, Aristotle, Machiavelli, Hobbes,

Locke, Rousseau, Hegel, Marx and Rawls.

The first of Vlavianos's eleven collections of poems in Greek appeared in 1983. His collection *Adieu* (1996) was translated into English by David Connolly and published in the UK by Bermingham University Press (1998), while the volume *Affirmation: Selected Poems 1986-2006*, translated by Mina Karavanta, was published by Dedalus in 2007. Volumes of his poems have also appeared in French, Italian, German, Swedish, Dutch, Spanish, Portuguese, Catalan, Bulgarian and Albanian translation.

Besides his own poetry, he has published five books of essays on literature and culture and has translated into Greek the work of a wide range of poets, to each of whom he has devoted at least one complete volume: William Blake, Walt Whitman, T. S. Eliot, Ezra Pound, Wallace Stevens, e. e. cummings, John Ashbery, Michael Longley, Anne Carson, Carlo Goldoni, Fernando Pessoa and Zbigniew Herbert.

Vlavianos is the founder and editor of the prestigious biannual literary Greek journals

Ποίηση (*Poetry*) and its successor *Ποιητική* (*Poetics*), which between them have been published for twenty years. Even in crisis-ridden Greece, *Ποιητική* is better produced, in terms of content and physical quality, than most poetry magazines in other countries, with sales of about 1000 copies per issue. Each number, running to more than 300 pages, contains new Greek poetry, translations of poetry from all over Europe and America, and original and translated essays on poetry.

Vlavianos's poetry crosses genre boundaries and contains self-referential, auto-biographical, essayistic and philosophical elements. His haiku are as difficult to categorize as his writing in general, and they present booksellers with the dilemma as to whether to place the book in the poetry or the philosophy section.

Vlavianos has borrowed part of his title from Bertrand Russell, and I would like to think that this book – the first volume-length history of western philosophy in haiku form – would have appealed to Russell's sense of fun. Indeed,

Vlavianos's wit and humour are perhaps more English than Greek. His haiku are often hilariously funny, but at the same time they succeed in conveying the history of western philosophy to the reader in an extraordinarily concise and unexpected way.

In my translations I have managed, with very few exceptions, to preserve the 5-7-5 syllable structure of the haiku. This was difficult, because English words tend to be shorter than Greek ones, and I had to avoid inserting padding that was necessary for the versification but undermined the pithiness of the expression. I hope you will have as much fun reading them as I had translating them.

The English translations of the ancient Greek quotations accompanying the first ten poems are from G. S. Kirk, J. E. Raven and M. Schofield, *The Presocratic Philosophers: a Critical History with a Selection of Texts* (2nd edn, Cambridge 1983).

Peter Mackridge
Oxford, December 2013

哲学

1. THALES

c. 620 – c. 540 B.C.

[falling into a well while he was observing the stars and gazing upwards]

Gazing at the sky,
you're bound to fall in the well.
Searching for water!

2. ANAXIMANDER
c. 610 – c. 546 B.C.

[for they pay penalty and retribution to each other
for their injustice according to the assessment
of Time]

The Big Bang? Hubris!
I'll put things in order. Time?
There's infinity!

3. HERACLITUS
c. 600 – c. 540 B.C.

[you would not step twice into the same river]

So it wasn't you
who entered the river twice.
It was someone else.

4. ANAXIMENES
c. 585 – c. 528 B.C.

[He said that the material principle was air and the infinite.]

Oh, I'm fed up with
infinite airy nonsense!
There I go again!

5. XENOPHANES
c. 570 – c. 475 B.C.

[But if cattle and horses or lions had hands, or were able to draw with their hands and do the works that men can do, horses would draw the forms of the gods as horses, and cattle like cattle, and they would make their bodies such as they each had themselves.]

If a skinhead were to depict God he would put a ring in His nose.

6. PYTHAGORAS
c. 570 – c. 495 B.C.

[he enjoined abstention from beans either because they are like the privy parts, or because they are like the gates of Hades]

How repulsive are those pulses! They remind me of hungry pussies.

7. PARMENIDES

c. 510 – c. 450 B.C.

[What is there to be thought must needs be: for it is there for being, but nothing is not.]

Whatever you thought exists. Thus it follows that nothingness exists.

8. ANAXAGORAS
c. 500 – c. 428 B.C.

[And since these things are so, we must suppose that there are many things of all sorts in everything that is being aggregated, seeds of all things with all sorts of shapes and colours and tastes]

What a thing is mind!
All it wants to do is sow
the seeds of gossip.

9. EMPEDOCLES
c. 490 – c. 430 B.C.

[When Strife reached the lowest depth of the whirl, and when Love comes to be in the middle of the vortex, there it is that all these things come together to be one only]

It's all for Love that
I'm falling into Etna –
to put an end to Strife.

10. ZENO OF ELEA
c. 490 – c. 425 B.C.

[that in a race the quickest runner can never overtake the slowest]

I'd much rather eat
a bowl of tortoise soup than
a dish of jugged hare.

Even though Zeno wrote about Achilles and the tortoise, he is thinking of Aesop: PM

11. SOCRATES
470 – 399 B.C.

I am the wisest,
despite having never
penned a single line.

12. DEMOCRITUS
460 – 370 B.C.

Plato's a very fine individual – he would atomize me!

There is a play here on the double meaning of the Greek word *atomon* (literally 'indivisible'), which means both 'individual' and 'atom'. Democritus is considered to be the father of atomic theory: PM

13. PLATO
427 – 347 B.C.

[The Republic]

That cave is fitted with all mod cons. It even has television!

14. ARISTOTLE
384 – 322 B.C.

[Nicomachean Ethics]

Eudaimonia:
that's the aim. (It helps if you've
flunkeys and a yacht...)

15. EPICURUS
341 – 270 B.C.

[Ethics]

Sex? I'd rather not!
None of that moaning in bed.
Celibacy, then!

16. SENECA
4 B.C. – 65 A.D.

[De brevitate vitae]

The madman's fiddling
after setting fire to Rome.
It's time to get out!

17. MARCUS AURELIUS
121 – 180 A.D.

[Meditations]

If you stoically
adapt yourself to your fate,
you will live nobly.

18. SEXTUS EMPIRICUS
160 – 210 A.D.

[*Outlines of Pyrrhonism*]

I've done away with
the dogmatics. Now I live
imperturbably.

19. TERTULLIAN
160 – 220 A.D.

[*Apologeticum*]

Plato and the rest
to the flames! I swear by the
Trinity. Amen.

20. ORIGEN
185 – 254 A.D.

[*De principiis*]

I'm a castrato.
I compose these arias
and sing them to Thee.

21. PLOTINUS
205 – 270 A.D.

[Enneads]

You'll become one with the One as soon as your soul takes wing to heaven.

22. AUGUSTINE OF HIPPO
354 – 430 A.D.

[De libero arbitrio; De gestis Pelagii]

Free will, Pelagius,
like that pelagic bird,
hangs heavy round your neck.

23. BOETHIUS
480 – 525 A.D.

[De consolatione philosophiae]

Any moment now
I'm going to lose my head. But
I'm philosophical.

24. AVICENNA
980 – 1037

[The Book of Healing]

The First Principle is God. Everything has a pre-existing cause.

25. ANSELM
1033 – 1109

[Proslogion (Discourse on the Existence of God)]

Since the concept "god" exists in the mind, then God exists. It's simple.

26. ABELARD
1079 – 1142

[Theologia]

I can see a horse,
but I can't conceive of
an abstract horseness.

27. AVERROES
1126 – 1198

[The Incoherence of Incoherence]

I wedded Islam
with Aristotelianism.
That's some matchmaking!

28. MOSES MAIMONIDES
1135 – 1204

[Guide for the Perplexed]

You need to follow
the via negativa
if you're seeking God.

29. THOMAS AQUINAS
1225 – 1274

[Summa theologica]

Prima mangiare,
poi filosofare!
That's life's Summation!

St Thomas's biographers note that he used to devour such large quantities of food that the monastery's carpenters had to cut a semi-circular piece out of the refectory table in order to accommodate his sizeable belly.

30. JOHN DUNS SCOTUS

1266 – 1308

[Ordinatio]

He exists. He must exist. God, I mean to say. That's what I believe.

31. WILLIAM OF OCKHAM

1288 – 1348

[Summa logicae]

My frugal razor's
sharp enough for the flabbiest
of unshaven necks.

Ockham's razor is the methodological principle whereby, between two equally satisfactory interpretations of the same phenomenon, the more complex one is likely to be mistaken, while the simpler is likely to be correct.

32. NICCOLÒ MACHIAVELLI

1469 – 1527

[The Prince]

Are you a weakling?
They will annihilate you.
You've got to be feared.

33. MICHEL DE MONTAIGNE

1533 – 1592

[Essays]

Knowledge stands with its heavy, stony legs buried deeply in the sand.

34. FRANCIS BACON

1561 – 1626

[Novum organum]

I have invented
the scientific method.
Voilà! Now use it!

35. THOMAS HOBBES

1588 – 1679

[Leviathan]

Life is the motion
of extremities. Collision is
inevitable.

36. RENÉ DESCARTES

1596 – 1650

[Discourse on Method]

Am I asleep? Can
it be that I am dreaming
that I am thinking?

37. BLAISE PASCAL

1623 – 1662

[Pensées]

Want to take a bet?
If you lose, you'll roast alone
in the Inferno.

Pascal's wager is the proposition that the believer has nothing to lose if it turns out that God doesn't exist, whereas the unbeliever will end up in Hell if he's wrong.

38. BARUCH SPINOZA

1632 – 1677

[Ethics]

I'm grinding lenses
to avoid rendering account
to the synagogue.

Spinoza was excommunicated by the Portuguese synagogue in Amsterdam: PM

39. JOHN LOCKE

1632 – 1704

[An Essay Concerning Human Understanding]

The mind is just a
clean slate, tabula rasa.
Born stupid, die dumb.

40. GOTTFRIED LEIBNITZ

1640 – 1716

[Monadology]

"My little monads do not have any windows." [Or curtains either!]

"The monads have no windows through which anything can enter or leave" (Monadology). For Leibniz, "every soul is like a separate world, independent of every other thing except God. Not only is it immortal, but it preserves within its essence the traces of everything that happens to it". These "separate worlds" are what Leibnitz later named "monads".

41.GEORGE BERKELEY

1685 – 1753

[Treatise Concerning the Principles of Human Knowledge]

Whatever can be perceived has real existence. Otherwise it hasn't.

Except of course minds…

42. FRANÇOIS-MARIE AROUET [VOLTAIRE]

1694 – 1778

[Candide, ou l'Optimisme]

Jean-Jacques? He's crazy! Bon sauvage? He can't make a Tarzan out of me!

A reference to Rousseau's view that man was free and happy when he was still an irrational being rather than a social one.

43. DAVID HUME

1711 – 1776

[A Treatise of Human Nature]

The sun is setting
today. Will it tomorrow?
It may do. Who knows?

44. JEAN-JACQUES ROUSSEAU
1712 – 1778

[Discourse on the Sciences and Arts]

Civilization
has made us into its slaves.
Back to the jungle!

45. ADAM SMITH
1723 – 1790

[The Wealth of Nations]

Invisible hand
manipulates the gold strings
of the free market.

46. IMMANUEL KANT
1724 – 1804

The mind's a laptop. We can all surf happily due to the software.

Unlike Hume, Kant believed that man can understand his experiences because the conceptual categories have been installed (as we would say in the language of computers) in his brain: quantity (unity, plurality, totality), quality (reality, negation, limitation), relation (subsistence, causality, reciprocity) and modality (possibility, existence, necessity).

47. EDMUND BURKE
1729 – 1797

[Reflections on the Revolution in France]

Rationalism
in revolution's service
is all-destructive.

48. JEREMY BENTHAM
1748 – 1832

[Utilitarianism]

One Christian martyred for thirty thousand Romans: a tasty morsel.

According to utilitarianism, an action is right if it contributes to the achievement of the greatest possible happiness for the greatest possible number of people.

49. MARY WOLLSTONECRAFT
1759 – 1797

[A Vindication of the Rights of Women]

I'm a hyena
in corsets and bustles. Men,
beware of Mary!

50. JOHANN GOTTLIEB FICHTE
1762 – 1814

[The Vocation of Man]

The pure self alone (and not Kant!) is what creates knowledge of the world

51. G. W. F. HEGEL
1770 – 1831

[Reason in History]

Human history
has reached its ordained end.
Long live the Kaiser!

52. ARTHUR SCHOPENHAUER
1788 – 1860

[The World as Will and Representation]

With baroque music! That's how I'll silence you, formidable Will!

Schopenhauer believed that the only way to escape from the will was by means of baroque music; it is the only kind of music that does not summon up the world of phenomena.

53. JOHN STUART MILL
1806 – 1873

[On Liberty]

Am I bothering you?
No? Then I will eat as much
pudding as I want!

54. SØREN KIERKEGAARD
1813 – 1855

[Either or]

You may hang yourself, or not, but you'll certainly come to regret it.

55. KARL MARX
1818 – 1883

[The Communist Manifesto]

Heroic Custer. [1]
Bloody savage Sitting Bull. [2]
Hollywood Western. [3]

1. Thesis. 2. Antithesis. 3. Synthesis.

56. CHARLES SANDERS PEIRCE
1839 – 1914

[The Essential Peirce]

What's pragmatism?
To die in destitution
for a woman's sake.

Peirce was dismissed from Johns Hopkins University, where he taught mathematics, because of a scandal regarding his personal life: his enemies alleged that while teaching at the university he was cohabiting with a woman whom he had not yet married. He died in extreme poverty.

57. WILLIAM JAMES
1842 – 1910

[Pragmatism]

What's pragmatism?
To reckon the cash value
of every truth.

58. FRIEDRICH NIETZSCHE
1844 – 1900

[Twilight of the Idols]

My work has driven
me mad – hammering away
at false idols.

59. GOTTLOB FREGE
1848 – 1925

[Sense and Reference]

Words give names to things.
But while doing so they
evoke a feeling.

60. EDMUND HUSSERL
1858 – 1938

[Phenomonology]

"I abstain": placing
experience in brackets,
I'm able to know.

61. JOHN DEWEY
1859 – 1952

[How we Think]

Whatever functions
in practice is true enough.
All you need's a test.

62. HENRI BERGSON
1859 – 1941

[The Two Sources of Morality and Religion]

The quality of creative emotion. You must focus on that.

63. MAX WEBER
1864 – 1920

[The Protestant Ethic and the Spirit of Capitalism]

Martin Luther was
the chief originator
of capitalism.

64. BERTRAND RUSSELL
1872 – 1970

[The Problems of Philosophy]

Forget your Philips.
William of Ockham's razor
gives a closer shave!

65. G. E. MOORE
1873 – 1958

[A Defence of Common Sense]

When I raise my hand
I can see it move upwards.
Therefore it exists.

66. LUDWIG WITTGENSTEIN
1889 – 1951

[Philosophical Investigations]

Can I make the fly
come out of the fly-bottle?
That is the question.

67. MARTIN HEIDEGGER
1889 – 1976

[Being and Time]

You're not only a
human being but Dasein.
Spend your Zeit on Sein!

68. RUDOLF CARNAP
1891 – 1970

[The Logical Structure of the World]

Have you bent Hume's fork? Then I guess tonight you won't be eating dinner.

"Hume's fork" denotes the distinction between analytical and synthetic statements.

69. MAX HORKHEIMER
1895 – 1973

[Eclipse of Reason]

Gaze at the eclipse
of reason, but make sure you
wear your black Ray-Bans.

70. HERBERT MARCUSE
1898 – 1979

[One-dimensional Man]

Want to get into
your jeans? You're going to have to
suck in your stomach.

71. GILBERT RYLE
1900 – 1976

[The Concept of Mind]

If you say "I'm angry",
it can only mean one thing:
"I'll smash lots of plates."

72. HANS-GEORG GADAMER
1900 – 2002

[Truth and Method]

Do read Paul Celan.
The kernel of truth resides
only in language.

73. JACQUES LACAN
1901 – 1981

[Écrits]

I resurrected
Freud and was crucified by
some of his pupils.

Lacan's controversial views resulted in his expulsion from the International Psychoanalytical Association in 1963.

74. KARL POPPER
1902 – 1994

[The Open Society and its Enemies]

Comrade Plato wants
to shackle you to his ideas.
You'd better watch out!

75. THEODOR W. ADORNO
1903 – 1969

[Minima Moralia]

When you hear of many
moralia, be sure to
bring little baskets.

The poem is a variant on the popular Greek expression, "When you hear of many cherries, bring little baskets." The title of Adorno's book ("The Smallest Ethics") is itself a pun on a work on ethics attributed to Aristotle entitled Ἠθικὰ μεγάλα ("The Great Ethics", known in Latin as *Magna moralia):* PM.

76. JEAN-PAUL SARTRE
1905 – 1980

[Being and Nothingness]

Feeling nauseous?
Maybe your existence is
lacking in essence.

77. HANNAH ARENDT
1906 – 1975

[The Human Condition]

If you submit to
totalitarianism,
you'll be a hangman.

78. MAURICE MERLEAU-PONTY
1908 – 1961

[Phenomenology of Perception]

Within the world and
only within it can a
man say who he is.

79. SIMONE DE BEAUVOIR
1908 – 1986

[The Second Sex]

You were not born for the boudoir. Neither are you only a female.

80. WILLARD VAN ORMAN QUINE
1908 – 2000

[The Pursuit of Truth]

Lack of identity
removes the essential ID
from your entity.

81. CLAUDE LÉVI-STRAUSS
1908 – 2009

[*La Pensée sauvage*]

The structure of all of the world's mythologies is universal.

82. SIMONE WEIL
1909 – 1943

[Gravity and Grace]

Communism and barbarism are alike: they wear the same bow-tie.

83. A. J. AYER
1910 – 1989

[Language, Truth and Logic]

Each proposition, including this one, must be either true or false.

84. ALAN TURING
1912 – 1954

["Computing machinery and intelligence"]

I was the man who broke the Enigma Code, but now they've broken me.

While working at the Government Code and Cypher School at Bletchley Park, Turing cracked the hitherto indecipherable German Enigma code. In 1952 he was found guilty of committing a homosexual act, and he took his own life two years later.

85. ALBERT CAMUS
1913 – 1960

[The Myth of Sisyphus]

Will you kill yourself?
No? Then give the stone a shove
to make it go up.

86. DONALD DAVIDSON
1917 – 2003

[Inquiries into Truth and Interpretation]

Do words have meaning?
Yes, in the sentences which
you articulate.

87. JOHN RAWLS
1921 – 2002

[A Theory of Justice]

Inequalities
in the system? If they help
the poor they're OK.

88. THOMAS KUHN
1922 – 1996

[The Structure of Scientific Revolutions]

With every change of captain, you find yourself on another planet.

89. PAUL FEYERABEND
1924 – 1994

[Against Method]

In the sciences
anything goes. Principles?
Rules? There aren't any!

90. GILLES DELEUZE
1925 – 1995

[(with Félix Guattari) *What is Philosophy?*]

Whatever you say conceals within itself what you cannot express.

91. MICHEL FOUCAULT
1926 – 1984

[Words and Things]

Truth and falsehood are
nothing more than illusions.
Language masters all.

92. NOAM CHOMSKY
1928 –

[Syntactic Structures; Language and Mind]

All languages have
a universal grammar.
Just ask your children.

93. BERNARD WILLIAMS
1929 – 2003

[Ethics and the Limits of Philosophy]

You've wasted a lot
of time on theorizing.
Get yourself a life.

94. JÜRGEN HABERMAS
1929 –

[The Inclusion of the Other: Studies in Political Theory]

Talkativeness is good. It might get us somewhere in the end.

95. JACQUES DERRIDA
1930 – 2004

[On Grammatology]

The meaning slips down nicely. It uses the tongue like a playground slide.

96. RICHARD RORTY
1931 – 2007

["The fire of life"]

I would have found the thread of life if only I'd become a poet.

Rorty published his essay "The fire of life" in *Poetry* magazine in 2007, shortly before his death.

97. ALAIN BADIOU
1937 –

[Manifesto for Philosophy]

I don't invent truths.
I filter them through the sieve
of what I call "events".

98. ROBERT NOZICK
1938 – 2002

[Anarchy, State and Utopia]

Don't I own myself?
Then it's legitimate to
pocket what I can.

99. GIORGIO AGAMBEN
1942 –

[Homo Sacer: Sovereign Power and Bare Life]

Homo sacer or
homo sucker? The Law can
strip your body bare.

100. MARTHA NUSSBAUM
1947 –

[The Fragility of Goodness]

Living is fragile.
Sophocles knew it too well.
But Plato didn't.

ABOUT THE AUTHOR

Haris Vlavianos was born in Rome in 1957. He studied Economics and Philosophy at the University of Bristol and History and International Relations at the University of Oxford. His doctoral thesis, *Greece 1941-1949: From Resistance to Civil War,* was published by Macmillan (1992).

He has published eleven collections of poetry, including *Vacation in Reality* (2009), which won the "Diavazo" Poetry Prize, and *Sonnets of Despair* (2011), short-listed for the National Poetry Prize. Dedalus published *Affirmation: Selected Poems 1986-2006*, translated by Mia Karavanta, in 2007. His latest book is an autobiographical novel, *Blood into Water.* He has also published three books of essays and has translated in book form the works of major European and American writers such as: Walt Whitman, Ezra Pound, T. S. Eliot, Wallace Stevens, e. e. cummings, John Ashbery, Anne Carson, Michael Longley, William Blake, Zbigniew Herbert and Fernando Pessoa.

His books have been translated into numerous languages (including English, German, French, Dutch, Italian and Swedish) and many of his poems have appeared in European and American journals and anthologies

He is the editor of the influential Greek literary journal *Poetics*, and teaches History and Political Theory at the American College of Greece.

ABOUT THE TRANSLATOR

Peter Mackridge is Emeritus Professor of Modern Greek at the University of Oxford and a visiting professor at King's College London. His books include *The Modern Greek Language* (OUP, 1985) and *Language and National Identity in Greece, 1766-1976* (OUP, 2009). He has written the introduction to *The Collected Poems of C. P. Cavafy* in the Oxford World's Classics series (2007). He has published translations of novels by Pandelis Prevelakis, stories by George Vizyenos, Alexandros Papadiamandis, Kostas Tachtsis and Yorgos Ioannou, and poems by C. P. Cavafy, George Seferis and Titos Patrikios. His books in English have also been published in Greek translation.

Dedalus Press

Named for James Joyce's literary alter ego, the Dedalus Press is one of Ireland's longest running and best-known literary imprints.

For more information visit **www.dedaluspress.com.**

"One of the most outward-looking poetry presses in Ireland and the UK"
—UNESCO.org